The Daily Prescription – Little Shades of Soul
Lisa Khan – Author

Copyright @ 2023 Lisa Khan

All rights reserved worldwide. All rights as Lisa Khan. No part of this publication may be reproduced, distributed, or transmitted in any form or by any means, including photocopying, recording, or other electronic or mechanical methods, without the prior written permission of the author, except in the case of brief quotations embodied in critical review and certain other noncommercial uses permitted by copyright law.

The author guarantees all content is original and does not infringe upon the legal rights of any other person or work.
www.lisakhan.com www.thedailyprescription.com

Book Typeset – Lisa Khan
Layout, Cover – Summer-Whitton Schluchter
Biography – Bill DeYoung

ISBN: 979-8-218-06571-3

The Daily Prescription
- Little Shades of Soul

For You.

*Billions of people,
Unique are your fingerprints.
Go make your mark
On the WORLD.*

*In times of negativity,
rest assured someone else is feeling positive
for you.
The universe is balanced...*

**To enjoy life
to the maximum,
you must presume you
will live forever.
However, seek not to
be disappointed if you don't.**

It is not necessary
to walk ahead,
and behind is way too far.
SIDE BY SIDE IS perfect.

Approach each
new day, as if it
were your last,
and honesty & joy
will pave the way,
and soften the road.

*If you smile often enough,
it will eventually become part of your daily routine.*

True happiness can only be found, when you realize where it is hiding within you.

*If you are asked what do you do for a living,
tell them,
I flourish.
And when they ask where do you live,
tell them,
Where I am loved...*

If you want to see a

blessing,

look in the mirror.

*Don't wait,
Stop collecting dust.
Brush yourself off.
There is time enough
for dust.*

Listen to the brain
Be grateful to the soul
Respect the heart.

The brain is
designed to keep
you safe,
*listen for it's
wisdom echoing*
from your heart

*When words
escape you,
Say the kindest
thing you can
think of.
It will serve
your heart well.*

Why be a Garden Variety When you can be a Sunflower.

*<u>You will never live an abundant life,
If you are busy seeing other peoples achievements as a reflection of your loses.</u>*

When you make

friends with the earth

You are never alone.

Your eyes are the
window to your poetry
Live a poetic life
Life is poetry

Ignore the whispers,
They are silent words
without a purpose.
The ones that smile
while speaking,
deserved to be heard.

*Rest easy,
yesterday is gone,
tomorrow is yet to be.
If you stay in the
NOW
You have
WON.*

You are not going to
break *my dear,*
you merely need to bend...

You walk down a
happy road when you
see the differences,

and accept them.

Find something that makes
you feel ***positive***.
Then find something that makes
you want to **share** it.

*Understanding
how to stay truly
present, is possibly
the best gift
you will ever
receive.*

Perfectionism is merely an image to save face.

Grow and make progress, *stay humble.*

Wish for nothing else

but time.

Without time,
You are nothing.

*Life is made up of musical notes.
Play the base,
discover the melody,
and there, you will play.
the **sweetest** of tunes.*

*The deeper
the soul,
The brighter
the heart,
The stronger
the spirit.*

The nicest people
like you for who you are,
not who they want you to.

There is nothing more pleasing to the eye than a smile.

It is $positively$ *contagious.*

- *Before you go*
- *make sure to plant a seed.*
- *A message in **someone's heart**.*
- *So, they may encourage others to grow.*
- *Igniting an abundance of love to flourish.*

You are never too much.
If you find yourself being too much,
Then they are not enough.
Remember you are someone's
right amount of everything.

Intelligence is a
powerful Gift,

when *balanced.*

Yet pointless when
misplaced.

Time is the most valuable asset you have. Don't waste it on the ego.

The body may slow
you down.
But the heart is
forever young.

I think of the most beautiful
thing about a person, is
the way they are capable
of making you daydream with a smile.

Even when they are not around...

*Find
someone who
finishes your
sentence,
and you,
will always
have
a flow
of communication.*

Love > Fear
A simple equation.

Your choice...

Life is the teacher that gives you the on-going project.

For us to grow together,
Fear cannot be
entertained.
Fear is the driver of hate.
Fear is the divider.
Fear will hold the reins;
Preventing the flow.
We must let fear take a
back seat,
and be
driven by **love**.

Your existence was
foundered on **love**.
To show **love**, is merely
a pinch of salt.
You must become **love**
Should you wish to participate in
the ingredients required for living

Never let anyone tell you that
you are letting them down.
You are not letting them down.
Their expectations of you
are letting them down.

WHEN YOU ARE ENCOMPASSED IN LOVE, YOU WILL WANT FOR NOTHING.

Stress does not come from the things you are doing.
It comes from not doing the things you like to do.

On rising, when you
open your eyes,
remember
someone else is
closing theirs for
the last time.
Gratitude always.

*DO NOT WAIT FOR SOMEONE TO TURN ON YOUR **INNER LIGHT**. TURN IT ON **YOURSELF**, IT WILL SHINE THAT MUCH **BRIGHTER**.*

Made in United States
Orlando, FL
11 July 2025